The Hills of Holland

The Hills of Holland

Poems

Esther Schor

Archer Books
Los Angeles

Published in 2002 in the United States by
Archer Books
P. O. Box 1254
Santa Maria, CA 93456
www.archer-books.com - info@archer-books.com

Distributed in the United States by
Midpoint Trade Books, New York, NY
www.midpointtrade.com

First Edition

Printed in the United States

Cover image: A Malay, Native of Bencoolen, T. Heaphy and A. Cardon
from *The History of Sumatra* by William Marsden (London: Longman, 1811)

Cover and interior design: JTC Imagineering

Library of Congress Cataloging-in-Publication Data

Schor, Esther H.
  The hills of Holland : poems / Esther Schor.-- 1st ed.
    p. cm.
  ISBN 1-931122-08-3
  1. Sumatra (Indonesia)--Poetry. I. Title

PS3619.C454 H55 2002
811'.54--dc21

                    2002027937

for Walter

ACKNOWLEDGMENTS

I am grateful to the editors of the following publications, in which several of these poems first appeared, some in earlier versions:

"Fireflies," *Kelsey Review*
"Leap Day," *National Poetry Competition Winners 1996*
"Opera Without Words," *The Jewish Quarterly, Michigan Quarterly Review*
"Guggenheim Abstract," *Michigan Quarterly Review*
"The Works of Galla Placidia," "'My tooth broke today,'" *Sequoia*
"Alef," *Judaism*
"At Dove Cottage," "Shap Abbey," *Times Literary Supplement*

For help of many kinds, thanks to John Burt, Anne Barrett Doyle, Paul Muldoon, James Richardson, and Jonathan Wilson. Saul Bennett has my appreciation for being a dream of a reader. John Taylor-Convery and Rosemary Tribulato of Archer Books saw my manuscript into print with care and discernment; I have been lucky to work with them.

CONTENTS

I

Opera Without Words

ANDROMEDA (*The Baleful Head*)

after Burne-Jones

At first light the weird sisters
falcon on the precipices

sharing a picnic of brie and pickle
and under Ethiopian stars, the fickle

Cassiopeia lies in Cepheus' arms.
The briny god concedes her charms

in every glittered wave, and on the strand
toning his biceps, curling granite

Atlas ignores the mackerel sky.
Pegasus kicks in the belly

his *grandes gestes* unsung; shirred
clouds lounge above the leisured

courts inlaid with mother of pearl.
Danaë's an ordinary girl

fair and fey and full of trust
unacquainted with Zeus's lust;

sepia-toned, the Gorgon
tosses writhing plaits, a virgin

learning stitches, doing sums.
Andromeda cocks an ear, runs

a toe against the font—a lute
in the western reaches of the orchard?

Tart breeze at bay, a drizzle
verging on rain, the well quicksilver

and Perseus, oblivious.
Uncoiled, Medusa's

moans attain an acid pitch,
ledges of air in a bruising rush

of shriek and wing. And now he lifts
the lidded prize, and clasps her hand, as if

to say *I can already see the night
your heavenly face shines down.* She might

look away, but without being told,
bends her neck to scan the cold

reservoirs of his achieved desire.
Then what does he see there?

Andromeda, ravished and surprised,
captivated by her own green eyes.

HAWTHORNE'S HOPE

You wait but it comes again,
a baby's knuckle, a palsy

a hazelnut shaken from side to side
within the abominable chest

you rest your cheek on the cool
lacquered plank, so close

a feather brushes by—
promise, promise, promise

hereafter, after, after—
and what good is a lid for

but lifting, you say to Epimetheus
who knew you would all along

since he saw you cradle one arm
tenderly in the other, the first time

you touched yourself.
Now Hope's taken wing

it makes a little difference,
cerise wash in the sky, a darker

timbre in his voice, viola
to cello. What to expect,

the caress you craved
all night on your pallet? A bell?

A pear? *a something beautiful
hereafter.* Epimetheus' wounds

swell and weep, so clear
she'll come to grief. Troubles steal

into grey creases of the forest,
hard to make out

among the blades of Egypt grass,
as though Rackham

had scissored the Fates
for the Tanglewood children

to happen upon later
in their quaint woolen stockings

and flowery names—Periwinkle,
Cowslip, Primrose—still too young

for tutoring, for all the other tales.

THE LATE BATHERS

Many little lies create a great truth.
—Bonnard

The ball of her foot, immersed to a dainty
parenthesis, in a basin you'll tip and drain,
     burden with pestles and whisks,
     on the mackerel tiles

of Le Cannet, beside a clawfoot tub bought
from a knifegrinder in Rue Eucalypte, a hovering Jew.
     Born Marie, she called herself Marthe
     and *I'll be here awhile* sang in the peach

curve of her cheek, grey eyes scratched in
with a chicken bone; a daub of ochre, later.
     And she, so easily pleased—a calico
     hooded in sheets, a mongrel nursing a sop—

threw the marceled curls of Renée into the grate
stabbed at the canvas until ash swirled like water
     back where it came from, desire
     squandered on love. A pumice stone,

a window opened by hand, then olives
silvering, a sagging upholstery of clouds
     rent by a cypress, now Marthe immerses
     a broad flank, a hip. Her breasts rise

as they sink, a range volcanic, lost, while overhead
finches of pleasure gather—a flitting blue, a skitter
     of gold. Around her neck,
     serenity closes a silver chain.

She opens her eyes, to see yours
closing; closes them to see
     what you will see there afterward.

OPERA WITHOUT WORDS

For Rhea

i

The day he gave her the *get*,
the sheytlmacher said *we'll go for blonde*.
In Borough Park, magnolias preened

amid the pigeons' Yiddish
and all the way to Suffern terminal,
an exile from the married land,

she dreamed the tame victrola by her feet
spun madly round the center of its pen,
a black dog hot for its own black scent.

After tea and busperfumed eclairs,
we closed our eyes in unison.
She took a needle to music, like a seam

that was always coming apart: *Grand Themes
of the Great Composers; Opera Without Words.*

ii

I reap, among the cabbage roses of the pillowcase,
the scent of Shanghai Carp, of West Lake Duck
in the rushes: lemon grass to cut the sweet

swimming flesh. Thrifty, rustic,
we made a meal of it, wandering condiments
just out of reach, our five fortunes, illegible.

Each night I lose them this way:
the children go back where they came from,
through a torn screen door a dog shuts

with his nose, bred to leave. Reversed,
they seem to wave us on, their kisses sting.
Reports deceive; never ask *how was school today*,

don't say at the easel, what *is* that?
He'll say *Good;* she'll say,
A house. At the scent of clay,

bicycles fretted, dreaming of rust.
Again you'd let it rain,
as though you'd had, all along,

a sure way to tell percale from muslin,
to translate the Norwegian girl's diary
on the day she wrote all about you, because

she failed to say what it was like to dream
in English, to have eaten so many verbs.

iii

We couldn't get over the saucy hip
on Donatello's David; a newborn calf dropped in hay,
blind and pink as a hawthorne. What could not

get over us: creosote in the Star Ferry's wake,
suburban moonlight treading door to door,
evangelical, dopey. The stuff novels are made on,

a neckline lower than low, breasts in relief, a nipple,
scored, fingered. Once again, I become the tongue
in your mouth, what I might say what you might say,

spring rain wiping the desert. And nothing, nothing
beating between your ribs but heart.

iv

In Kowloon, all brides eat beggar's chicken,
and I was no exception. A cake in tiers,
raspberries shipped from Macao. As long as you

threw confetti in lieu of rice, as long as you signed
right to left, it took. After their day jobs,
before their night jobs, boys in dragon boats

strewed the harbor with pistachios,
drumming to combinations of waves.

v

Chelm had its theories, and Warsaw:
you hear one ear at a time—
but only the sound of your ears;

the moon is a slice of cake—
the moon is a butter knife.
What we had to know, we learned,

the way hitchhikers from Montreal
in the absence of priests and maps
learn somewhere west of Tulsa

to spend afternoons at the Safeway
among aisles of frozen orange juice.

vi

From a virgin, the oldest question:
Can a tampon get lost inside my body?
Next month she'll ask again, as though

the circular were code, as though jewelweed
weren't the remedy. A cramp in the last leg
of our journey. As we finally master our cameras,

what claims our admiration?
Modest capitols, decorous ads:
cars for prawns, ovaries for men.

On the backs of bridges and towers, you write
in white space: *I am at home here. No here. No here.*
When learning the beards on national stamps,

kindly refer to your guides: *Florilège, Keepsake, Brown's
Compendium of Deer.* The thirsty waves, the tragic drums,
arias of salt. The token says (if you hold up your change

to the light, if you read Chinese):
The Last Nickel Ride in the World.

GUGGENHEIM ABSTRACT

Tell me your story, the turpentine said:
introduce yourself,
gesture,
do one of us in. The mayflies' whine,

the rasp of toads, spores peppering
invisibly, the turf; my *once again*
became
this time. How tenderly the red sun sank,

how the moon swiped at the droplets. A man
just left of Frank Lloyd Wright said
travertine,
one finger on *reverse.* The tape loops back

to a plenary address, conventioneers
in velvet galleries. Our work's in progress:
in the beginning,
Kandinsky, and after, Malevich, and then, and then. . . .

What terrible ends they kept from us, singed dolls,
argosies of smoke,
moraines;
and such flat feet, such sexy afternoons in small, Saigon

hotels: *Le Vendôme, Les Quatre Chats.* Weather, slightly foxed—
a drizzle loiters at the corner, blued;
neat Piet
cruises his mind. Now we near the hanging gardens,

give or take a story, what was forest clears,
and in airless elevators, icons shatter
to the hum
of fans. It's before we know any better, the hour

of garters, nylons, menthols, permanents,
in lieu of pockets, welts, an alligator
clutch.
I'll take grey before black, and wait

till Kelley's greens have drained a bottle of chartreuse.
After twelve suspicious fires, they renamed paper
ash.
The Italian girl in platforms gapes—

Millecentonovantasei!—a skull
sprung from Yorick, dipped entirely in pitch,
minutes
of the shadow cabinet. Ryman's still

unravished brides await their picture
grooms who sail tonight from Crete for
dowries
stained with ouzo. Two shades deeper than Macon

a Rothko falls in rectangle love;
you heard me right, my dear, you saw that it was
good.
The day before he died, Zero Mostel stood

where a nippled fruitwood breast gleamed
under the high hats, while several
bushy
thoughts bounced down the ramp into a checker

cab en route to Ozone Park, but that's another story.

LA SFORZA

Lucantonio Cupani, her priest
biographer, parades
Caterina's penances:
maceration, naps on stone,
fasts to quicken

a Sienese namesake
who gave up wine, bread,
water, finally
the cherished turnip—
martyrdom's gorgeous

austerities.
The vellum riddled
with La Sforza's recipes is gone;
a copy rendered
in demure, clerical script

offers cures to the infirm
or simply curious,
since curiosity's
a type of infirmity
as Thomas Trollope knew,

his talismanic quill
seduced by Levantine
mummies, Cornish ghosts,
second-sighted
Turks. Afternoons,

he'd take a good cigar,
a beaker of milk,
back to the study
on a floor too lofty
for the rank *malaria*

and write, sip, puff;
after Neufchâtel
(Rousseau's
faux Grasmere),
in lieu of milk,

a bowl of heavy cream
with a grassy tinge.
"To drive a pallor
from the face: shredded
myrrh steeped a day

in muscat wine,
guarantees carnations
in the cheek." Orangewater
for blotches on the neck,
a remedy to whiten

teeth, and one to redden
gums. One, near the end,
"for multiplying silver"
as though Madama
aped the Jew she'd lured

from Bologna's ghetto—
how, Tom Trollope
barely surmised—to do
the Forlivesi's "little bills,"
douse St. Peter's silver

till it bloomed.

HORACE

Horace, I read somewhere, taught Latin Greek,
taught it to sing. Horace put Latin
out of step, put Latin out

like a hound for the night, till it bayed
at a crust of moon, and sniffed
the air for brine, where it learned

how we ply the dark
from the provinces back to the isles.

THE WORKS OF GALLA PLACIDIA

Late June, the sister of Honorius would rage
against the solstice: *Day worn on a bias,*
impossible to anchor with the fibula.
Trying, I have more than once drawn blood.

Midsummer, she was more composed; *the moon*
sang softly on a bed of wheat. Their sordid secret
strained them, yet they never gave it up.
In autumn, when *Jupiter cast stars into the sea*

like pearls, Honorius moved the court
from Rome to Puglia. She didn't balk;
hadn't he promised her
an alabaster table, porphyry floors,
thirteen-hour lamps? She liked
their privacy, and planned to start
a longish piece on Pliny's verse.

But like all homeowners, she was beset
with mice and leaks; *Scirocco thrummed*
the awnings, sun baked
her brain. She piled quarterlies
on the onyx mantlepiece and left
a life of Hecate
on a low divan, unread.

One made one's choices, in the end,
depending on one's taste in genre.
In the *History* she never wrote,
Empires fell like light.

II

Fireflies

FIREFLIES

You see them by not looking: damp sparks
in the grass, cool glitters
in the elms. Even Patsy
noses the air upward, rising, arcing
gone. This morning, in the library,

A Child's Book of Insects:
First flash, males,
how often says how dire; then females,
how soon after
says everything else—

all preferences known
in a flash: who's who,
who will, who won't,
what will or won't work
out. The Chinese ate them for longevity,

but they're above eating, their business,
knowing when to disappear.
Bitter, but frogs gorge
and gleam. Last night
unmoored a dream of you

afloat in the Dead Sea
reading an aura of
newspaper. I ask what rhymes
with *sand, moon, tears*
you say my name, name, name.

What glows in the ocean?
Sand? Moon? Tears?
That sound you hear,
what you thought were waves,
my name, cresting on rhyme,

cresting on dream. Late
fireflies flare at the hedge,
drop from sight. At your house
all night the roses bloom,
a white the beginning of light.

PUNCHLINES

Netted, aquiver, citronella's all we remember
the sun by, now night pools in the air. A handful

of patio days till he's a Sunday call,
all running heads. No nuns roll downstairs,

no one asks *who's there* when we
knock-knock. In the mind's parade,

orphaned punchlines shuffle and strut:
crosseyed priests believe in Dog

poodles read torah, rabbis eat ham,
fringed epaulets, a dazzle of trombones.

Ten summers ago in Maine,
the platinum lake gave nothing away,

shallow and deep all one, he'd leap
from wherever he stood, out

of his depth, our fault—we found differences
hard to explain. On fingered waves, his name

skipped like a stone. He's Freud's little pauper
still, a holdout for salmon and mayonnaise.

And as you turn the volume down *(Marcel,*
said the farmer's wife, *voici un homme),*

the mailman slips out the door, tasselled, fezzed—
"you told me to fuck him for Christmas!" —

and just tonight, the sky's an old shag carpet
taken up to show the spangled taste of gods

who've since moved on. Scolded, consoled,
Susannah's back (she followed a rabbit

into a neighbor's pines) and turns it up;
she likes it loud and towel-hulas

to the crickets' beat. Tell me a joke
that's not on us. Sue yells to a saltine moon,

the sky walks into a bar! We laugh
as August spits into autumn's eye.

HAYAKUTAKE

This frozen clump of grit, mantled, sunbound, plays a little havoc
with the clouds, the tail of its travels vague, offhand. The epics all agree:
to damage heaven takes more
than malice. At one am his silly
cock a doodle do alarm

earned watering a neighbor's cryptomeria, gives out a crow
and crows again; he yawns, zips up, *jeune perdu*
back in the suburbs, stubbled,
flushed. Between his teeth,
a second dark's inside.

He punches the sky, *you measure like this,* his fist no bigger than a plum
and we exchange a glance, our toppled empire's currency—
don't leave him alone with the stars
to unbuckle Orion's belt,
dishevel the Pleiades.

What Adrienne carried, Park Slope to Torcello, in an oatmeal box
taped shut and magic markered *BONE MEAL SUPPLEMENT*
just as Henry had requested
dissolved in Italian water.
So much for smiling Quaker

subterfuge; she loosened the top and out they swirled
in breezy ashen arias. Venetian monks took meteors for the return
of all agglomerated sin
to earth; it's nothing
you bump to the end of,

sin, it's coda on coda on coda. But there, between what dissolves and what's
     opaque,
the souls of boys and comets meet, eye to tail, self to shadow, substance to
     accident.
I know this about secrets:
whatever scatters, matters.
I'll tell him then,

ten years from now, when he takes the whitest sheets in the house,
balls up his shirts and jeans and specimens of quartz
a box or two of reeds,
postcards of resorts.
When we close our eyes

the speed of light slows to precisely the speed of darkness.

LEAP DAY: FEBRUARY 29, 1996

For Sally and Joe

Bonus twin, midnight born,
    thirteenth roll in the baker's dozen,
        a day for sambas in the nursing homes—

last dance, ladies' choice! My grandmother
    picked husbands like honeydews
        in the Safeway, where you smelled dung

in the meat aisle, chickens among eggs;
    in sawdust, the footprints of shoppers already home,
        scraping a carrot, boning a fish.

Once a century, it slips through our fingers; next time
    we'll know it was earned, like the seasonal love
        of a neighbor. The other years—

missing? misplaced?—overdue checkup, book drawing fines,
    forgotten lesson. *Today I'll grow extra*
        says Jordy, measured against the fridge before school

and after, *a definite quarter inch taller!*, which I'd gladly give
    to his stunted cousin, two years sick;
        and to Michael, who can't say *I want,*

the day's extra words; and these round hours—
    half to his friend with leukemia, half to mine with AIDS.
        February, a fever you said in Latin class,

while out the window—spring? snowdrop?
    winter? snow? By a shade,
        more is less than enough, but today

after years of scares and tries, Beth had a fine baby girl
   (*She'll have her days and nights mixed up for weeks*),
      a tiny cry an inch from the phone. And afterward,

I hung up a Japanese scroll
   to set something lucky between us
      and what might yet come between us:

six white cranes leap
   into a golden sky.

THE WHISTLE

It switches a mighty magnet on, kicks slow
       to a beat, shining torsos needle
to the ladders of the pool

while a scant, dusky form
       saddled in gold trunks
drifts, face to the sun.

White-beaked guards,
       barely fledged, swoop down,
bind his spindly wrists, limp ankles

shining brow to a plank.
       How exquisite their ministry
this strapping and winding

not remedy, preparation; no CPR,
       no mouth-to-mouth, no cartoon
gush since he's already dead

a Pharoah's son afloat on his palanquin
       down the fecund waters of the Nile
past an empire of mourners

season-mourners, day-mourners
       paid, unpaid.
A quiet in the air, cool, ancient,

embalmed. On this bank
       I weep for the dynasty
soak the gauze in linseed oil,

ready the canopic jars
       for the bright fruits of his organs
and when they loose the straps

he leaps like a small canary-god
      for a high five with the guards
since it was only a drill, since the PA blares

Senior waterobics in two minutes!
      Grey hair tucked in lycra caps, the elders
bob like festive, pungent eggs.

ALEF

For Robbe

Sunday, far north
  the broad air
leafless, farmstands
  hunch at the roadside
boarded, murmur
  a *brucha* for last fruits—
last pumpkin, last apple,
  last week;
the chill Sabbath
  kept at bay
returns to the schoolroom.
  A moment before learning
what do we remember?
  lamed, a lamp
mem, a mouth
  taf, a table, a tack
as though all letters
  bloomed into things
as though God were wandering
  the vineyard, blessing
the heavy vines. But God's become
  forgetful, we've all noticed
the change; frost cracks
  the folding husks
binds the soil
  where we planted
marigolds; my daughter paints
  in crimson streaks
alef, akimbo, unimaged:
  it says nothing
because the sound it says
  is invisible

ITALIAN LESSONS

Islands larger than Sardinia take *in*—
Madagascar, Greenland and Australia—
smaller, a compensatory *a*—
Ischia, St. Croix. *What about Japan?*
Suddenly an atlas
lay open between us

for Paola was exacting and exact.
Like Padua's anatomists, she pinned
to my brain's gray paraffin
(English-scored and Russian-pocked)
wriggling idioms
flayed prepositions

a fibrous sequence of vascular tenses,
salutations muscular—*Amore,
Onorevole, Egregio professore*—
eventually, bifurcate subjunctives.
Jack, her live-in
Aberdonian

had left a Scottish stain on
Paola's silken, seamless English
spun a year or two in Cambridge;
it nubbed and snagged and darkened
at the edges,
and she fretted—

something was unraveling.
The day she left, Chianti sipped
from Dixie cups, she asked
what's shade and what is shadow?
Shadow goes;
shade's traveling.

ORCHID PAVILION

When I ask, you pause
        over one lone
dumpling, spoon heaped
        with jewel chicken:
Whose poems do I like
        these days? Tsing Tao
floods your throat.
        Can't recall the last poet
to raise my hopes, or even
        give me a tilt. From deep
in a pocket, a handful of wrinkled lace
        for a late-March blast
of snotgreen prose. We drink our
        tepid tea and pay the check,
skipping our fortunes. Yours
        would have said:
You are the wonderful thing, my dear
        and it's no picnic either.

TWO FOODS I HATE

Chisel, balloon, osprey
Ode, curio, foolscap, parch
Busker, mutiny, seawrack, quire
January, March.

Slipper, purse, davenport
Timber, mosaic, predella, hussy
Savannah, barbican, fraction, spine
St. Simeon, St. Lucy.

Boneyard, whelp, repeater
Vise, tooth, crêpe de chine
Son of a bitch, mother of pearl—
Limes and lima beans.

SO FAR

Not two inches long, barely grey
the mouse I found lying midcarpet, still
and unaroused. Not normal,
I thought, taking its tail the way

I'd seen a landlord do, using
only two fingers; I was a student.
Accident? Incident?
Call it a finding, a losing.

Not grey at all, a tiny ear
pink, nearly, a pale petal
before you see it, a matter settled
before it matters. Almost clear

of import, weightless. You told me
mice stick madly to perimeters,
one panic after another
and said *sick, maybe*

newborn? What sent it from margin
to middle, it won't tell
and I, born forty years ago, and well
am left to imagine

some longing fiercer than my own
in a far gentler thing.

FIRST SNOW

For Sandra

I dressed you for summer: white linen suit,
tangerine blouse, scarf of silken mint—
sherbet colors, you'd have said,
a good choice for forever

What was I thinking? gulls
scritching, moaning,
on the humid verandas
of eternity

you, on a chaise longue
sipping iced coffee under star palms
splayed fingers
between your eyes and the sun

putting up with the prayers,
the lid, dirt falling stone by stone,
then home again, rested—
tea, boiled eggs, cake.

I say *first* again,
I purse my lips. Snow
shows me my errands,
I'm beyond doubt.

False teeth, false breast
Etruscan replicas
a lock of my hair
bones and baubles gone to ice—

once, I couldn't think your death would last.

THE SNOW GHOSTS

For Daniel, Jordy, Susannah

Where the rise slopes into brambles,
you can make them out:
girls in pink hats coming down,
knees tucked into roasting pans,
boys in balaclavas
on flying saucers. Here before us,
when our architect was a kid
drawing planes, when maples
strode to the ridge. We took half a hill
to house our boys, now swallows
build dwellings
out of ours, they nest
in concrete crumbs.
Something more than a bird
wants back whatever we took.

A man who knew
said *your trees are distressed,*
their crotches are weak.
We thought the woods
would settle us. Deer come
to the glass, tawny,
skittish, whatever
they seek must still be here;
one limps, another
lags, as though
fear were too hard
to remember, after all this time.
Easier to lap at the brook
where the ice gapes,
where you still hear water.

In snowpants, the boys could pass
for trees, thick, dark,
unyielding; *not deep enough*
they yell, as though
the cost of joy were gravity.
How much more can they take
than we can give?

The snow ghosts wave
from the rise
fall onto their sleds, whoosh
through the house; for them,
it's always deep enough.
That chill down your back
as you flip the eggs,
your neck stiffening
over the paper, they go

right through you

thread between the trees
like something blown down, down
from somewhere clear out of sight,
and clearing all the flood lines,
ten years, fifty, five hundred.

III

Cumbria

For Walter and Ray

i. AT DOVE COTTAGE

The morning after we bombed Hiroshima
Helen Darbishire awoke in Sussex
convinced by a nightmare Dove Cottage
would be the Japanese ground zero

as if Rydal Mount, its terraced
greenery cascading over Rydal Water
and field of daffodils planted for a daughter
by the churchyard, buttery and blessed

were but a late surmise, and one returned
before the end to weatherbeaten, timbered
walls and narrow panes, to chambered
intimacy coveted and spurned,

far from an eminence. William's idea,
a passage from garden to study, to avoid
a sooty parlor where Coleridge tried
dipping Schlegel into English tea.

Still in the larder, a page of the Gazette—
a young man of excellent qualities
seeks a position for the summer holidays;
still in the cabinet, Dorothy's blunt skates,

John's dull razor; still before the embers
a whiff of wet fur off Scott's springer spaniels,
thirty-seven shivering animals
sharing three names like a bowlful of custard:

Ginger, Pepper, Mustard.

ii. SHAP ABBEY

The Abbott of Furness sold out to the crown
not so the Abbott of Shap; nothing spared
but an arm of transept, a backbone
of cloister, a tower's shin. Through arches
a glimpse of boys playing bowls, laundry aired
in the dappled shadow of larches.

Two miles away, in the Bampton road,
the tiny chapel of Keld, raftered
and thatched, a thousand years old.
A leaflet given out at mass:
"Can YOU recognize a solvent sniffer?
Is YOUR child using drugs?"

It's after the ravage, plunder, swagging
the armfuls of lead and limestone
carried by torchlight to wagons,
harnesses barely holding the horses,
terrible bells taking the sky down,
saints lying in pieces—

too late for lauds and tierce and prime,
for scathing lanterns shone in the eyes
of urchins bedded on straw and stone.
King Stephen's nineteen winters,
the Abbot of Shap couldn't forgive
(*one leaves through the portal one enters*)

but when kindling blazed and the mead purled
he was known to say: *King Edward lived
like an angel amid the squalor of the world.*

iii. HELEN ON BUSTER

Helen up from Suffolk in her Mini:
"The mother, you see, the mother was Bluebell
so all the calves were named with B's—

Brownie, Bonnie, Bert. Now Buster
was more like a pet, he came, let's see,
the spring of '93. What a scene when Bluebell ran

from the AI man, he fetched her down
at the piggery; nice, he was
but fit to be tied, and the pigs

squealed for hours. The boys,
well Nicholas, gave him his feeds
looked after him, groomed him

with the dog's brush. Had games with him—
got rough, I gave them what for, they still remember.
When he turned two, just this March

we sent him off to a man near Darley
down the A31, who sent him back
in steaks and mince. And was *he tasty! and tender!*"

iv. THE RUSSIAN CIRCUS AT KENDAL

Honking a Porsche, goggle-eyed Ramon
throws nuts and kisses to the crowd. Nitka's
tugged the door off, grinning, boombox hoisted
as the ringmaster—*NO NOISE!*—unplugs it.
Ramon drives slow enough to drown
a thimble of sorrow in shoesful of vodka.

Cadence of trumpets—interval. Selling floss
the girl who balanced fifteen crystal goblets
on a fingertip counts pounds and pence.
Her acne's bad; after feathers, sequins
and mascara, something's lost.
A lion tamer sells us raffle tickets.

Finale: Galinova and Konrad, so familiar
from the poster, riding stallions bareback
curve on curve around the ring
dressed as Huns, perhaps, or Tartars.
Whipcrack, and two brilliant flags unfurl:
Mother Russia, Union Jack—

a real crowd pleaser, and a megaphone
implores, *Come back and bring your friends!*
We shuffle off to the rented car,
interlopers and itinerants,
here just long enough to know
a bargain at two quid a head.

v. "MY TOOTH BROKE TODAY. THEY WILL SOON BE GONE."

—*Dorothy Wordsworth*
Grasmere Journals, May 31, 1802

One hazel nut intended for your pie
would not be mashed.

At tea you served yourself,
after William, after Coleridge,

the third wedge of pie
the fourth slice of a knife

then, musing on the substance
of the word *nutmeat*, you bit

and broke in two the tooth
gone grey and dead in Somerset,

that looked back from the mirror
like a woman smaller and older than you.

As voices rose into steam
you fingered the fragment from your mouth,

and set it on the saucer's rim
like a mirror laid face down.

vi. HELEN ON DOUG

Helen in the garden, over tea:
"Just a word now, really; *husband.*
Nothing between us anymore,

not for years. Those days in art school,
another world, always ink on his hands;
I'd scrub them nights with Lava

but he left fingerprints everywhere.
Camberwell, it went downhill;
back past ten on his motorbike

knackered, a look at the paper,
and off to bed. Even the pre-eclampsia,
took no notice, what you'd call

a workaholic. Never drank,
him, not one for the pub
(oh, in the country, the occasional crawl)—

they adored him at Time-Life.
But going freelance, and up to Suffolk,
his bloody mother's bloody house,

one bad idea after another. The boys, don't ask;
he'll promise a day at Safari Park, end up
phoning from Milan.

Come Nigel's birthday, I took them down;
lions came up to the window,
they barely noticed and all the way home

it never came up. (No big cheese,
lions, when dad's forgot
again.)
              Well, here's to absent friends.

Once they gave me the sack
at the *Weekly*, I stood for the Council—
you know the rest. Paid work

after a fashion; thankgod they compensate
mileage, running hither and yon
three nights a week

up late over zoning reports
up early cooking them breakfast, eggs
and sausage and toast.

Mind you, I'd leave him if somebody came along;
where it went, I don't know
but once it goes, it's gone."

vii. EDINBURGH: THE SCOTTISH NATIONAL WAR MEMORIAL

Just beyond the Castle barracks, cobbles
round a parapet commanding views
east to Holyrood and black St. Giles;
north, Scott's spindle looks about to topple.
Inside the apse, a granite frieze of thistle,
the Highlanders' *Sans Peur* and the Royal Navy
cenotaph: *They have no other grave than the sea.*
A bust of Captain MacConnachie, killed by a missile

at Ypres, hushes the boom of the one o'clock gun.
You'd leave but for the names: Dardanelles, Loos,
Gallipoli, Gibraltar, Palestine,
Struma, Persia, Mesopotamia, Marne.
Below crossed swords, draped in Lancer tartan,
a chill so sharp it cuts July in two.

viii. SCOUT SCAR

Before we came, it had already healed:
north to south three miles long;
below the ridge, a bleachéd field,

rubble fences licked by a tongue
of the Irish Sea, the Morecambe Sands.
Daniel complains about the sun

moans for the jug of ribena, hands
me his camera—"Take me at the edge!"
I've had enough of his demands

of his boyish poise on this rocky ledge,
warn him back to the path
as if to say this limestone wedge

is, after all, a scar, a swath
of earth risen up to the sky
to tell the news about death,

how it comes and goes, how a cry
becomes speech, turns to a whisper.
Not a relic of pain gone tough and dry—

a circular stain left by a visitor.
The jagged scar on Daniel's face
became what he said, as much as his lisp or

even his cockeyed tooth; *nowhere I'm safe,
not even with you.* Like the surgical curve
on my mother's breast, or the crescent I trace

on your back, they unswerve
in the mind, stay straight
as a biblical plot: God loses his nerve

before Abraham. From this height,
you'd think all scars belong to the earth,
each a map that reads us north

and south: *you were already here,*
you have passed this place.

IV

The Hills of Holland

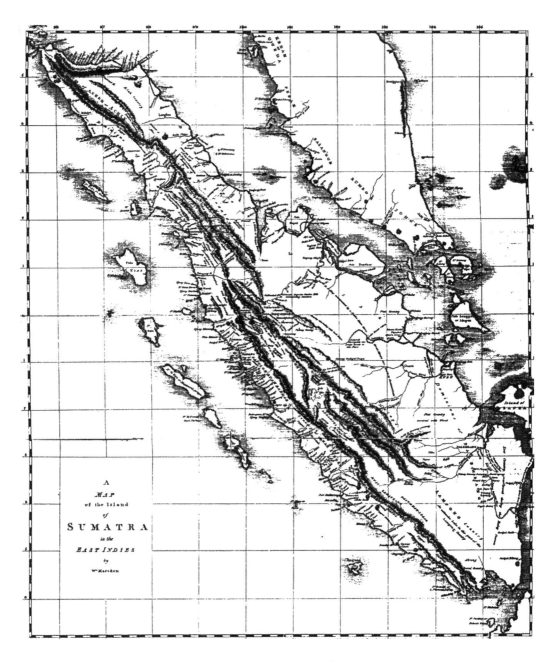

A Map of the Island of Sumatra in the East Indies by Wm. Marsden, published in 1810

i. William Marsden, Aldenham, Herts. November 1835.

They have no theory of the scale. My ear
discerns six whole tones, frequent
flatted thirds (*vide* Bengal ragas,
Galway airs), decisive preference
for the minor key.
                    Malay, all vowels
and liquids, makes a music of its own,
Mandeville's *Italian of the east,*
ripe to verse's touch. At *bimbang,*
boys of nine or ten extemporize
for hours, legends unspooled
to proverbs' knots. Their choicest form
is called *pantun* (when brief),
or else *dendang,* an undulating
phrasal rush the ear
takes back a moment, till it ebbs away.
Peculiarly, it quits just as it starts.
One night I gave Wasub, God rest his soul,
a pantun of my own—Dyer's *Grongar Hill*
rendered in Malay; it might have been
a Welshman's scorn upon his face,
and *katta katta saja,* all he ventured—
chicken-chatter.
                    They write on paper,
rude pens honed from anau twigs,
characters furnished by the Saracens,
words for butter, milk, and musket borrowed
from the Portuguese.

ii. Nakhoda 'La-uddin, Bantam House,
Royal Crescent, Bath. April-June 1829.

In the Name of God, the Compassionate, the Merciful.

To the honor of Nakhoda Muda,
beloved father, beloved son of Nakhoda Makuta, born on Banjar isle
under the Sultan of Bantam, may Allah preserve his memory!
Who made the seven heavens and the earth,

who fashions us from clots of blood
splits the seed and the fruit-stone, and in whose praise
I tell my father's story, the child Tayan and the lordly Kei Damang,
the man who shed names

like a gecko. My grandfather lay
in life's shallows, his voice a chip of shale: "Praise Allah
and avoid to contract debts. If a man greets you,
let your greeting be better than his.

Cut timber, fish, dry more pepper plants
than Sultan needs. Owe nought except to Allah, who winds up the sun
that will outrun the clocks." A dusty voice, he blessed the Day
when men shall walk in broken bands

to be shown their labours.

Honour the mothers who bore you: Radin, O daughter of Paduka,
a dream of copper shoulders, teeth white as tanjong petals.
By *semando,* Tayan married Radin Mantri,

a simple fee of twenty Spanish dollars
and a buffalo. Each night she dreamed the orchards of her childhood,
the cashew-apples of the monkey-jambu trees
woke to the taste of tears

until her womb foreswore its fruit.
And by the second waning moon, she and my father
followed her yearning heart back to the bay
of melons: Samangka.

And from this wife came four,
two daughters and two sons, Wasub and 'La-uddin;
and from the concubines in Bantam, two sons more—
abandoned, disowned.

The bamboo house
swayed and creaked, a vast cradle rocked by trees.
He built the ladders strong; by night four children clambered up.
Between the births

of my two sisters, hill-troubles. All knew
the Abungs' customs: a skull for the father of the bride
full of gold and silver beads, a skin of arrack drunk
to good fortune and good hunt.

I saw my uncle's headless corpse
veiled by white ants, devoured before the evening
rice had boiled. Nakhoda Muda

called a Council of War,
five days the local *pangerans* gorged
on upland boar and dainties, bemoaned a lack
of knives. Till sampans arrived

barely afloat, piled high
with Spanish muskets from the Sultan of Bantam.
At dusk, amid treefrogs' piping and the plovers' pips
the first report was heard—

the Abungs fled, but not before
Nakhoda Muda's anger flared among their fields.
Cassowary birds, maddened by the mingled scent
of sulfur and the flaming camphor pits

shrieked fire-fear till dawn.

My child's-eye met burns and blisters up and down
my father's legs; to reedy sulins and the beaten gong
of victory, they filled and wept.

iii.

Your entry in the *DNB* yields names and titles,
   titles, names: William Hunter Marsden,
      born at Verval, County Wicklow (quite

by accident; your father, having burst
   a fortune in the Bubble, quit Lincoln's
      green unpleasant land and sailed for Cork,

a week on Irish suds).
   Secretary of the Admiralty (retired),
      Past Treasurer of the Royal Society

and Fellow, Asiatic Society, Calcutta;
   Past President, Society of Antiquaries
      (1819, when Graham succumbed

to cholera en route to Istanbul);
   Recording Secretary, Literary Club
      and Honorary DCL, Oxon, a happy

culmination for a Balliol boy
   who, Cicero-stricken, found himself
      on Boxing Day of '79 at Gravesend,

stowedaway on board the *Ranelagh*
   and Java-bound. And made Malay
      his Latin and his Greek.

Close the book; I seem to see you now,
   rolling a currant between thumb and palm,
      firm, unripe, eager for spring

while the unpartnered hand,
   the one you've lost the use of, dreams
      the blushing nuzzle of a rambutan.

Here's shade enough for midday
   scribbling, gravelled walks circuitous and broad;
      with so much said, perhaps one yearns

to say a simpler thing before the end,
   how schist blinked up and down
      the eastern face of Mount Ophir, how light

came through the amber berries of the pepper plants.

iv. Marsden

My *History* (which in its third edition
I consult) begins with vulgar errors:
atrocious customs meat and drink
to them, the old adventurers,
the Polos, Pigafettas, Mandevilles,
cannibals who on behalf of the
infirm, made choice of lesser torments:
suffocation, *then* a stew. To Ptolemy
a paltry Java-bis, or as he put it, *Java-dib*;
to Javanese, *Indalas*; to the Saracens,
who cast ashore Mahomet and his steed,
Al-Rami or *Lameri;* then (and here's
the boxing ring of etymology—
in this corner, Malay *semut,*
a large and scrappy ant, and opposite,
samatra, legendary Spanish squall)—
and then, Sumoltra, Samotra, Zamatra,
Samana, and in time, to all, *Samangka.*

v. ‘La-uddin

Enter your dwellings by their doors
and fear God, so may you prosper. And from each sleeve
of Kiria Minjan, the Royal Emissary, hung a silken dragon.
With iron claws, they bent my father

to the Sultan’s will, to judge
among breathing men. Radin swept between the sago trees,
and there Tayan heard petty squabbles of the pangerans.
Hours baked and crumbled

into dusk, shade pooled
and took him where the voices barely reached. When kunangs flecked the leaves
with sparkles nibbled from the sun, he praised *the fire whose fuel is men and stones*
spoke judgment and was done.

On a cold, damp isle, where old men
drink babies’ milk, I learned a word for my father’s gift,
what the English call their game of Sultans and Sultanas
robed in sleeves of darkness

and blood: *patience.*

vi.

A series of authenticated facts
   you undertook to gather and record,
      eight years, thirty-seven days of life

riven into halves of darkness and of light
   by the equator; the ancients built a village
      on the Line, better to beckon

a capable god. Travel five degrees
   northward, land runs out; and south,
      the same, a perfect palindrome,

but for a handful of minutes. *Hence*
   the obscure predilections
      of the surf. It surges in inverse

proportion to the wind, attributed
   to inertia of waters equatorial,
      produced by the increased velocity

with which they spin, which mitigates
   a small, perceptible degree
      of gravitation. From land

you see the swells afloat
   upon their backs, the lifting,
      slender arms of foam draw on the softest

of horizons, varied as the shapes
   the fog assumes; you might be idle Hamlet
      stabbing at the air, but here, amid

the fetid dung of elephants, you glimpse
  a foal, a terrier, the plump cheek
    of a Wicklow girl who'd sailed for France.

Hence, waterspouts that clear a treble
  range of mountains, leeward to windward;
    hence, a swathe of havoc sharper than an axe.

That island to the east, where cascades fell
  and strove to rise again, it wore a crown
    of clouds. You tasted seven kinds of rain,

sucked the vein of liquorous palm, hoisted a nauseous
  cup at Pakanbaru springs: Brimstone Toddy,
    Harrowgate Hell. To keep it down,

the sulfurous mess, a chaser of arrack.
  Now and again, to the monsoon's whine,
    that blessed compote, tambaku and hemp

puffed through a water pipe Malays called
  ganga bang, in India, a *bong.*
    Marsden, some wet hours slid

from the pages of your *History,* some
  went up in smoke.

vii. ʿLa-uddin

Kiria Minjan—The Scorpion.
In youth, left for dead upon the scree (scampering
Abung, morning fire), a royal beak bent low to him,
a wide, covering wing.

It is the scorpion's nature,
as the proverb says, to sting; and so he did, the royal breast
he owed his life—*each soul, the hostage of his deeds*—
and filled his fist

with Cochin sapphires
from the cask of Ratu Bagus Buang. Fitted out
in Ratu's panchalangs, he plied his errand to Samangka,
where sea-cows feast on melon.

From spies, Nakhoda Muda
learned Ratu's plan: take one hundred captive in the barks,
parade the shamed Malays before Rejangs in sooty villages,
seduce them all with vows

to snap Batavia's stalk.
A Council called by night: Nakhoda Muda plied the drowsy pangerans
with promises, begged them to keep faith with the Sultan and the Dutch;
Wasub was sent, his son

and emissary, with pepper,
oaths and tidings to Batavia where in the lodge of Mynheer Sambirik
he met a foundling from Utrecht, indentured
to the Company.

In Tino's sharkfin eyes
rocked twenty weeks of waves, his mind tossed
beyond sleep. Like drying fish, on braided mats they lay
while Tino told his tales:

Epiphany, I clanged the frozen bells
from tower to turret, and clanged again, when suddenly,
Hoogstraaten kirk took wing, and up we flew

above the hills of Holland
fields lay like Turkey carpets
frozen lakes made O's

with silver mouths
saints from their portals turned the fields
to angelbroed, red tulips gaped

in snow. Skating children heard
a crack deep as the earth,
and all at once they sank

into the black heart of the mere.
Which saint took all the babes?
the grieving mothers asked, Was it the Father

or the Son? And once the kirk touched down
I never saw one step inside again,
nor heard a blessing

pass their unkissed lips.
Wasub whispered, *another.*
In a soft cheek, the bone worked.

viii. Marsden

Our recreations, mainly backgammon
and Irish, the occasional round of euchre.
Rabok, our servingboy, prepared a deck
stripped of underlings; all rank,
no file. Sundays we read Psalms
or Lamentations, a brace of Scottish
hymns in deference to our Primo,
MacLachan. The hour passed slowly
in pews hand-hewn from mahogany,
carven grapes and chalices
hard on our backs.
                                The rains came gentle on,
a morning sprinkle, dusky shower;
then jackal-crazy gusts. A great hand
spread its fingers over us, not a shutter
stayed in place. The downpour
seemed to course inside us till
we took it for the beating of our blood.

'Twas then Necessity, great mother
of et cetera unwombed the Fort Marlborough
Shakespeare Troupe, not, as widely rumoured,
I. Our debut, *The Winter's Tale, Or
A Congelation Devoutly to be Wish'd.*
To Moore I gave Leontes' role, and took
Polixenes myself; to Rotherhithe,
of open brow and decent mien, Camillo;
the rogue Autolychus went straight
to glowering Douglass of Strathclyde.

ix.

And she of *pinching fingers, paddled palms,*
   whose *life stood in the level of his dreams?*
      Who, *innocence for innocence*, inhaled

the air of sixteen years as in a single
   breath and let it out before the world's eyes?
      To him you taught your mother tongue, who took

between his plumstained lips and flawless teeth
   a line from Milton or a verse from Pope,
      and left it smoked in jaggri bark, kissed

with a scent of pergularia,
   all consonants, all rhymes dissolved
      in fluent hisses of the surf. Seven

years astride a teakwood bench
   as monsoons whined and waned, words tossed
      between you like a java-rubber ball,

Malay to English, English to Malay,
   all for your dictionary's sake. He never lived
      to see the book. Between its covers, cordovanned

and gilt, emboldened words like sentries ranged
   at intervals upon a ridge, between
      these sheets, the impress of his heart and soul,

faint as a watermark. Hermione
   went to good Wasub.

x. 'La-uddin

Nights on end, in Sambirik's lodge
the hurricano lantern burned. Stars sank their weary heads
on cloudy shoulders. Wasub, Wasub
recall the verse:

the dog pants if you chase it away,
and pants if you leave it alone. He thought he saw his mother's hair
dance in the flames, his father's sampans bob upon Samangka's waves,
as Tino's voice, slight as a girl's,

ravelled all ends to beginnings.

No sooner had they crossed
the Oosterscheide
than it began to swell and flooded

all the plains from Roosendaal to Zeist,
herring trapped in branches,
briny fruit. This was no ordinary sea,

but a vat of tears
cried by the Wolf-Queen, mourning
her torn Wolf-Prince.

Nakhoda Muda waited for Wasub. By day,
beneath the latticed shadows of a chinkareen, he scanned the waves; by night,
amid the keening waves, the stars. And when a new moon
whelped a squall

the sea's great mouth swallowed
sampans of plantains, broke ribs of panchalangs upon its back.
He knew the time had come to leave seafaring to his sons.
Sambirik was pitiless,

intent upon his meerschaum
and his concubine, but before a new moon rose again,
Bantam sent pitch-and-timbered sloops bearing
a title: *Kei Damang.*

And we paid homage to Bantam,
passed beneath the silken canopies where eunuchs burnished
silver betel-stands. *Does man think we shall never put his bones
together again? who draws out tiny fingers?*

and at the Sultan's knees,
my father bowed his head, renounced the boat, so as to keep his sons
from debt. The royal name, the title Allah destined
for his bones, that he prayed to take

into gardens watered by running streams,
he kept. Now he was Kei Damang.
Now Kei Damang was he.

xi. Marsden

A brief digression on the Rejang tribe:

They have no God. Their *dewas*
(*deus* bastardized) lurk
about ancestral graves, nameless
household godlings; and bound by equal parts
of apprehension and affection, Rejangs drink
only from wells of the dead; the hills
they cut their teeth on take them, toothless, in.
Had they a god, he'd wear a tiger's face;
he's *nenek*, ancestor, and not *machang*
(and never mind his taste for human blood).
They say he reigns in palaces of bone
thatched with women's hair. By night
(if Shanklin—or his whiskey—may be trusted)
they crouch beside the hogfoot-baited traps
set by the Company to save their necks
and when the beast approaches, whisper *nenek
mattoi, mattoi!—careful, death is near!*
lest his blood be on their hands.

Rejangs.

       The Battaak
tell how earth began: Princess Puti-orla
rode a white owl out of heaven: fearful
for his daughter's life, King Batara
visited his mother in the sea—
a brew of mud and flame, such was the milk
he drew from her both her teats; and thence he formed
the flaming ramparts of the world.

'Tis true, what has been said of the Battaak
(*vide* Di Conti, De Barbosa, Beaulieu):
they do eat human flesh, but as a mode
of shewing detestation of a crime; in the event,
the local *raja* must assent, dispatch
a square of cloth to cover the offender's face,
together with a dish of salt and lemon.

xii.

A Malay meets Allah everywhere:
  pillowed on his mother's thighs
     in the ragged seam between his wife's—

so said Wasub. Strange that a man of forfeitures
  and resignations (unwived, not wifeless;
     not childless, unfathering) should put it thus.

Well, Ramadan had left him parched and weak.
  And when the weary
     sun laid down his sack to sprawl

upon a barrowcloud, when palsied scriveners
  and junior clerks slept babu-style beneath
     the breadfruit trees, when heat-lashed shade

outhushed the heat—
  then you rehearsed your play.

xiii. 'La-uddin

As children loosen *mampalams*
with thumbnails, young men take a blade to *jacca* fruit.
I taught him how, the son of Captain Poer; he wore his parents like a hat,
his father's flaring ears, his mother's

bleachèd hair, but somehow dodged his temper
and her squint. Samangka's children feared him, as we feared Captain Poer.
Unasked, my father built them a henhouse and a pigeoncote;
they added rawcord fences

and a sty, then cleared
our pepper plants from view. There, servants nailed themselves a hut.
They called her, sweet Samangka (where melons give up sugar
to the sea), *Poerdorp.*

And how they came to be among us?
May the prophet and angels assist me.

Some say the Fiscal,
jealous of Damang, put forth a rumour—forbidden trade with Englishmen
had been resumed at Kei's command. Some said
it was a Tappanouli Corsican

one of d'Estaing's marauders,
who ran a Frenchmen's brothel in Bantam. Who knows the truth?
Trust ran aground between Samangka and Batavia.
To make amends,

my father paid Sambirik's fine
and for his pains, was taken prisoner by Captain Poer;
the Sultan, busy with his cockfights, let it pass.
And so they came,

my father's captor, Poer,
his wife and son and servantboy: a grey-eyed slender stalk of chaff,
a crumb of Dutch cheese.

The next tide brought Wasub.

xiv. Marsden

Such bickering, and such ineptitude!
Our Wicklow pantomime outShakespear'd this.
As Leontes, Douglass snorted, growled
and stamped, like a Sicilian buffalo;
and Rotherhithe, who looked a fine, if musclebound
Camillo, could not raise his voice above
a moth's.
            But *mirabile dictu*, by torchlight
in Bencoolen Hall, before a hundred souls
the centre held:
               Wasub played Hermione
to my adroit Polixenes, with all the grace
and bearing of a Queen
whose tender cadences pulled like the surf
at our astonished hearts, her *verily*—
indeed—*as potent as a lord's.*
Met with such grace of execution,
such demure and (dare I say it) womanly
aplomb as one would seek in vain at Vauxhall
or Tonbridge—I outdid myself.
When faint Camillo mumbled his *forbiddenly,*
I filled the air with rage and oaths, as if
my blue Bohemian blood had turned
infected jelly, my sterling reputation
to a reek. Indeed, MacLachan said
my hideous savor struck the dullest nostril
in the crowd.

And in the role of Time
I made my mark as well, begged reprieve
for *my swift passage o'er sixteen years*
with nimble capers and beguiling leaps;
and so persuasive was my mimic gaze
into a vaporous glass, they craned their necks.

Truly, I *gave my scene such growing*
as they had slept between.

XV.

And if *a sad tale's best*
   for winter, as your bard and namesake said,
      November gives you pause to watch the moorhens

knead the oaten skies of Hertfordshire
   to roost, before another month is out,
      beneath Sardinian eaves.

xvi. 'La-uddin

May Allah raze them
from the earth, Batavia, Muara Tanda, Poerdorp
and leave it scored and pitted where they lay.
On the Day of Days

men shall become
like scattered moths; the mountains, tufts of carded wool.
May those betrayed be succoured at the quinine springs
of Salsabil, which healed

the Prophet's pilgrim foot.

For years I kept this tale between my teeth for Wasub's sake,
how he tumbled out of time, as will the firedancing souls
who forget God made them

from bloody clumps of flesh,
who do not reflect on the camels, who heed the mischief of the slinking
prompter, *did he make you? You?*

how he pinned the doorway shut
with sago twigs lest a child watering the earth between her heels
might see a roil of arms and legs, unwombèd twins
aspill upon the ground,

mouth pressed to mouth,
as though the aching breath of life could be forsworn, the lamp
threw shadows of a giant cockchafer, upon the thatch
beneath the writhing stars

it heaved and twitched
in rhythms of its own, and *tinka, tinka, tinka* went its song. . . .

At Captain Poer's request,
Kei Damang and his sons followed in a praw
to pay a visit on Nakhodas at Croee. At Muara Tanda, wordlessly,
the Hollanders put in their ketch,

and burned MacLachan's lemon orchard
to the ground; a jagged line of stakes thrown on the dirt
unpinned a patch of England from the earth,
smoke took its ashen tale upwind.

They said, a glass of arrack
on the Captain's deck, *opla!*—boats winked together and apart.
And as we boarded, Kei Damang and both his sons,
they drew our krisses from us,

bound our hands,
and took us prisoner. Then Tino spat and went below.

xvii. Marsden

Our carver's excellence, indeed; Wasub
came honestly by wrinkles on his brow,
years of squinting in the sun.
Just as they never say their names, Malays,
they never tell their age, and truth be told
it wasn't clear he knew. I guessed he had
a dozen years on me, but then they age
with an alacrity untypical
of Englishmen.
           Which is to say
he looked the part: rice flour dusted
cheeks and shoulder, betel streaked his mouth
(*the ruddiness upon her lips is wet*);
with linen fresh unmangled, warmth hid
in its folds, I draped him, head to foot.
The pose he struck was not as we'd rehearsed;
head cocked, eyes wider than the night
we bivouacked below the Lasa Hills
and saw orangutans put up their mocking palms
to fire; what *evils conjured to remembrance*
left Sicily appalled were nought to those
that struggled for a kind of life in Wasub's eyes
and made him, lost in weeping, theirs.
And when the cue came—*you perceive she stirs*—
he shivered visibly, whose ear had shaped
the words into a romance of his own,
so still, Leontes stepped upon the bamboo pedestal
and held a hundred souls within his proffered hand

and only buckled shadows and the cicadas' rasp
prevailed to eke flesh out of timeless stone.

He took Leontes' hand and came, still weeping, down.

xviii.

What plied between his Allah
    and himself? You were never wont
        to say—I doubt you knew—

nor *make it manifest where he has liv'd*
    or how stol'n from the dead.

xix. Marsden

                Fifty years
have passed, and in Croee are some
who still say I played Time more grandly than
Bohemia; well, my temper's one part
philosophical, one part historical,
two parts dramatical. Besides, 'tis nature's
truth:
           Hermione shan't be wooed.

I bowed, struck the scenery and doused
the tusser wicks, but never told the denouement.
And Allah, bless him, is as mum as I.

xx. ʻLa-uddin

Three days and nights we lay on deck
in Spanish irons, Tino's narrow eye above his pistolet's black mouth.
Given a rats' nest of rotting cord, we plaited lines,
the sea's fist pounded out the hours.

And when they slew our buffalo,
the stink of roasted flesh rose from their terrible bimbangs,
the bones they hurled to sea
Samangka carried back to shore

on grieving waves.
I prayed *O break their skin with teeth, their teeth
on bones, their bones on rocks*, my father's head bowed
in prayers of his own

while Dutchmen spooned a pot
of layang-layang soup, Wasub stood in his irons, licked
his cracked and bloody lips and dived
between the parted fingers of the sea

xxi.

This little I know:
In the tin dish by his hammock,
Wasub concocted

rosemary and rue: a paste
of sago bark and orpiment, the first,
to dull his senses; the last to stop his heart

at which it failed. A week
he teetered on oblivion;
in lieu of physic or physician,

Chalmers' mumbled, Presbyterian
—*pray for his soul*—your midnights,
Marsden, and your noons.

Though not a pious man, you said
a blessing on his prostrate soul,
the heavy hours lay like guineas

on his heart. Afterwards
you never spoke of it, recovery
adequate to bring the dictionary

to an end. He'd changed, his eyes
wandered from the page,
an inattentive child

following a file of ants,
he scanned the ferns
for phrases once his own.

xxii. 'La-uddin

Praise Allah, then we ran amok

a savage clamor in the bow,
my father's dagger-bitten
flesh, Tino's elbow

cambered like a willow
on a lacquer box
bending, lifting, bending

Kei Damang's blood
slow to depart,
red streams down his arm, black puddle at his feet

and Tino's spattered
scarlet pinfeathers
on my two hands.

The boom of English canon
splintered Dutch masts, cracked ribs
of boats and men alike

and when I dived,
flesh bobbed for cormorants,
sank for sharks.

At Bencoolen they said
an English yawl en route
to view the scorchèd groves at Muara Tanda,

had pulled my brother from the sea,
laid him on deck. My mind's blade
peels back rumour's skin—

a chamois cloth
moistened with palm oil,
a level hand that swabbed

my brother's flaming face,
the face he opened eyes on
dim and kind,

mouth rounding words
he'd find his own
lips make

in days to come.

xxiii. Marsden

Fishing hookless
like the Achinese, we felt among
the *tuba* roots for carp, who *tuba*-dreamed
their way into our hands. Next, I thought,
a gazetteer of coastal islands;
Engano, Sanding, Pulo Triste, perhaps
a study of Japan; "next, *next;*" my voice
ran down his neck like summer rain.
From time to time, he told an old, cracked
Holland tale of wings and wolves. And thus
his mind's eye rounded the earth

until an early autumn fever brought
his glossary of heartache to an end.

xxiv. 'La-uddin

The next Indiaman to sway
out of Bencoolen harbor, bound for Good Hope,
St. Helena, and Plymouth, had me for freight.
When the Flood rose high

we carried you in the floating ark.

So ends the tale of Kei Damang, commissioned
by the Cardiff Orientalist Society, recorded by
his eldest son, at Bantam House, Royal Crescent, Bath

who never saw his father
and his brother into Allah's earth, but left
them bathed where waves lick clean the melon seeds
on Samangka's shores.

XXV.

In Nelson's wake, you rose to eminence.
  As Secretary of the Admiralty, you took
    the one-armed hero's obsequies

to your sole charge, raven crepe
  upon the stallions' skirts, gilded bosses
    on the catafalque. They said a baronetcy

lay in your neighbourhood,
  and they were wrong.
    Did bitterness or generosity

cede your pension to the crown?—
  for which the Parliamentary applause
    carried to Hertfordshire.

xxvi. Marsden

        The spines of all my books
are gilt: my *History of Sumatra,*
Corrected and Improved, flanked by
translations into German, French, and Dutch;
my catalogue of Oriental coins,
Marco Polo Englished; and a teakwood
bookstand built to order by a Punjab
joiner down in Potter's Bar, bearing
Marsden's Dictionary of Malay

in which, from time to time, I peer
as in glass and see, or think I see,
a face nor wholly mine, nor his,
but catching something of us both,
as though there passed between us
not eight years, but one word,
partly a query, partly an answer.

(All for my dictionary's sake.)

        This evening,
phantoms quicken in the library:
McMahon and Moriat, my Celtic
tragedy, stunted at Act Three,
a dozen brief Anacreontic odes
scribbled while he dozed, the *Coastal Gazetteer,*
barely begun; unpublished tracts
delivered to the Royal Society,
Beliefs and Customs of the Battaak Tribe.

And my *Comparative Analphabetic Guide*
to Five East Indian Tongues with Sanskrit
and Kashmirian Synonimaes?
It languishes, since my catastrophe—
thrown from a mare, sprawled in the Bushey Road;
I have attained an age, as Graham was wont to say,
when injury never leaves us where it finds us.

This has indeed become a winter's tale.

In March, a touch of apoplexy left me
some degrees remote from where I was;
my left hand's uncorrected, unimproved
my right, a widow pacing back and forth
upon a narrow pier, to catch a glimpse of sail
before it goes. I keep a spaniel, Raffles,
with me on my walks, and when it rains
I feed him points of toast with muscat jam,
a practice common in some parts of Wales.

NOTES

Guggenheim Abstract: Millecentonovantasei, 1996. The poem followed a visit to "Abstraction in the Twentieth Century: Total Risk, Freedom, Discipline" at the Solomon R. Guggenheim Museum, 1996.

Opera Without Words: *get*, a writ of divorce; *sheytlmacher*, a wig-maker.

Cumbria: With the exception of "Edinburgh: The Scottish National War Memorial," all poems refer to sites and topographical features in the county of Cumbria in the Lake District of England.
    At Dove Cottage: Helen Darbishire (1881-1961), co-editor (with Ernest de Selincourt) of *The Poetical Works of William Wordsworth* (Oxford University Press, 1940-49), is said to have initiated the microfilming of the Dove Cottage archives immediately after the bombing of Hiroshima. The story is probably apocryphal.
    Helen on Buster: *AI*, artificial insemination

Alef: *brucha,* a blessing.

The Hills of Holland: I have drawn on three sources: William Marsden, *History of Sumatra* (London, 1811); ['La-uddin], *Memoirs of a Malayan Family, Written by Themselves,* trans. W. Marsden (London, 1830); and the entry on William Marsden in the *Dictionary of National Biography* [DNB] (1921-27). The narratives of Wasub and Tino, of Wasub's work with Marsden, and most details of Marsden's sojourn in Bencoolen, are fictional. Quotations from *The Koran* are drawn from N. J. Dawood, ed., *The Koran* (Penguin, 1997); quotations from *The Winter's Tale* are drawn from G. Blakemore Evans, et al, eds., *The Riverside Shakespeare,* v. 2 (Houghton Mifflin, 1974).

About the Author

Esther Schor is a poet, scholar, editor, and Associate Professor in the Department of English at Princeton University. Her poetry has appeared in *The Times Literary Supplement, The Yale Review, London Magazine,* and other American and British journals. She was awarded the Joseph E. Brodine Prize and her poem "Fireflies'" has been nominated for the Pushcart Prize.

In addition to her duties at Princeton, she is a frequent contributor of book reviews to *The New York Times Book Review, The Times Literary Supplement,* and *The Star-Ledger.*

About the type

This book was typeset in Plantin. Designed for the Monotype Corpo-
ration in the early 1900s by F.H. Pierpont, Plantin is named for the
sixteenth-century Antwerp printer Christophe Plantin.

Book design, typesetting and composition by JTC Imagineering,
Santa Maria, CA.